TITANIC

What Really Happened

The Shocking Secrets Buried Beneath
The Waves

Phil Coleman

Table of Contents

Introduction

Thanks to the extreme popularity of James Cameron's 1997 film *Titanic* most people have a fairly accurate idea of what happened to the titular ship on the morning of April 15, 1912. Aside from the romantic plot between the main characters that was completely fabricated, the filmmakers took care to get the details of the ship, and the events of the night, more-or-less correct.

RMS Titanic was British shipping company White Star Line's most luxurious ocean liner to date. It was part of a trio of White Star ships known as the Olympic-class ocean liners, that included HMHS Britannic, and a ship actually called RMS Olympic. Titanic cost $7.5 million to build which, in today's currency, is $300 million.

At the time of its building Titanic was genuinely believed to be unsinkable. The ship could stay afloat with any two of its watertight compartments, or all three of the forward compartments totally flooded. It seemed impossible that the ship would sustain any injury that would cause the flooding of more than three compartments, as such damage was almost unheard of. White Star chairperson J. Bruce Ismay recalled, "I think the position was taken up that the ship was looked upon as practically unsinkable; she was looked upon as being a lifeboat in herself."

Even White Star's Vice President Philip Franklin backed up the rumors. When news of Titanic's collision with the iceberg got back to land, he made a statement saying,

"We place absolute confidence in Titanic. We believe that the boat is unsinkable."

Of course the rumors were just rumors. Titanic was made of over 40,000 tons of high quality building material. It may have been unlikely that Titanic would sustain an injury that would sink her, but she was definitely made of materials that would sink. So what exactly happened to Titanic, the so-called unsinkable ship?

The Accepted Story

Titanic set sail from Southampton on April 10th, 1912 on her maiden voyage across the Atlantic Ocean, to New York City. There were more than 2,200 passengers on board. Late in the calm, still evening of April 11th, Titanic struck an iceberg that created several devastating gashes on the starboard side. The damage occurred over a 300-foot area, and breached the first six watertight compartments.

Titanic could not stay afloat with that many compartments flooded. The hull slowly took on water and the ship began to sink bow first into the icy waters of the Atlantic Ocean.

Evacuation procedures were frantic and shoddy. While Titanic had enough lifeboats to meet legal regulations, the ship did not have enough lifeboats to rescue every person on board. The crew knew this but, to avoid a panic, went about trying to convince passengers to stay on board the ship rather than board a lifeboat. When the call for women and children only was sent out, many women decided to stay with the men in their party and wait for a lifeboat that would take all of them.

Many of the boats were not even at capacity when they were launched. Boat 7, the first lifeboat to be launched from the ship at 12:45am, had the capacity to hold 65 people, but only went to sea with 28 aboard.

Several passengers on board believed the stories about the ship being unsinkable. They saw no reason to leave the comfort of their cabins and head to a chilly deck to wait around for a lifeboat. Even those who did go to deck weren't too panicked at first, as they assumed the lifeboats would ferry passengers to awaiting rescue ships and return to collect more people.

Most passengers did not fully grasp the danger of the situation. Second class passenger Lawrence Beesley later said, "The great majority were never enlightened as to the amount of damage done, or even as to what had happened. We knew in a vague way that we had collided with an iceberg, but there our knowledge ended, and most of us drew no deductions from that fact alone."

As the morning went on Titanic continued to sink. The previously launched lifeboats were not returning to get the remaining passengers, and it was clear that there were not nearly enough lifeboats left on the ship to save everyone still aboard. People began to panic.

Survivors told stories of men dragging other men from remaining lifeboats to make way for women. There were confrontations with firearms. Officers were issued revolvers at 1am, and it only took until 1:15am for one to be used. Fifth Officer Lowe fired warning shots between a lifeboat and the side of the ship to stop men from attempting to board the boat.

There are numerous survivor accounts that allege that, as the last lifeboat was being prepared for loading, the confrontations become fatal. First Class Passenger George Rheims said, "As the last lifeboat was leaving I saw an officer kill a man with one gun shot. The man was trying to climb aboard that last lifeboat. Since there was nothing left to do, the officer told us, 'Gentlemen, each man for himself, goodbye.'. He gave us a military salute and shot himself." There is eyewitness evidence that this man may have been First Officer Murdoch.

Over a thousand people were still on board when the weight of the ship's stern became too heavy, and Titanic broke in two. The stern leveled out onto the ocean's surface once more, but was dragged down by it's tenuous connections to the bow. The two parts of the ship broke away from each other underwater and came to separate resting places on the ocean floor, 1,970 feet apart. Most of the remaining passengers died in the water of hypothermia while waiting for rescue.

Due to several confusions with passenger lists, it is not actually known how many lost their lives that morning. Some people cancelled their trips shortly before the ship set sail, but were still on the passenger list; some bodies were unidentified and could not be cross-checked with lists; some bodies were never found; some were travelling under aliases and were counted twice. Sir Walter Lord's famous book on the tragedy, *A Night to Remember*, puts the death toll between 1,490 and 1,635, approximately 800 of whom were passengers. Most sources say around 1,500.

Although the ship Californian was in the area at the time of the sinking, the crew did not come to rescue the survivors for reasons that remain somewhat mysterious to this day. Rescue operations were left to the Cunard ship Carpathia.

The three-and-a-half-day trip to New York on Carpathia was tense, cramped and uncomfortable. The rescue ship already had its own passengers aboard, leaving the Titanic survivors to have to huddle on deck. Many people were coming to terms with the fact that they would probably never see the loved ones they had lost or left behind again.

Survivor Ruth Blanchard remembers Carpathia as, "the saddest time of all. That was the time so many of the women who had been put into lifeboats by their husbands, and told they would meet each other later, realized that they would never see each other again."

Carpathia reached New York on a rainy Thursday, April 18th, 1912. Thousands of people had gathered to greet the survivors. Also present were Philip Franklin of White Star, and Senator William Alden Smith, who came aboard Carpathia to ensure J. Bruce Ismay and what remained of the crew would be present at the US inquiry into the sinking to be held at the Waldorf-Astoria hotel beginning the following morning.

This version of the story is widely accepted as fact. Many believe it was simply a tragic accident that caused the great unsinkable ship to find a final resting place at the bottom of the ocean. However, there are many strange occurrences surrounding the sinking that call into question the legitimacy of that tale. Alternative theories range from insurance fraud to assassination, and from political turmoil to the paranormal. With so much mystery surrounding the sinking we may never know for certain what really happened to the world's most famous ship.

The following stories are some other possibilities for what could have happened on that fateful night.

Major Players

Before getting into the theories it is useful to know the people who feature most prominently in the stories, the hand they could have had in a conspiracy plot, and what they had to gain from what happened to Titanic. Here are some of the key figures in Titanic history.

J.P Morgan

John Pierpont "J.P" Morgan was the owner of White Star Line, and features heavily in many conspiracy theories about the sinking of Titanic. He was an American banker who was instrumental in the creation of General Electric, The United States Steel Corporation, AT&T, and the Federal Reserve.

Morgan's company *J.P Morgan & Company* took on failing businesses and reorganized their structure and management in order to make them profitable again. This process came to be known as "Morganization".

Perhaps the most impressive example of Morganization is Morgan's plans to prevent an economic crisis of the United States government. In the 1890's the Federal Treasury was running out of gold and on the verge of defaulting. Morgan convinced President Grover Cleveland to buy gold directly from his bank to restore the surplus.

He also came to the rescue in 1907 when New York banks were on the verge of bankruptcy, and the country was once again in financial trouble. Morgan and his fellow extremely wealthy bank owners redistributed money among banks, managed to secure international lines of credit, and injected money into the troubled stocks of otherwise thriving companies. His aid and ingenuity eventually convinced the government to create the Federal Reserve.

As an American, J.P Morgan should not have been allowed to own Titanic, as it was a British ship. He could, however, own the company that did own the ship. In 1902 Morgan's shipping company International Mercantile Marine Co. (or IMM) absorbed White Star Line after Morgan threatened then-owner J. Bruce Ismay with a rate war.

Morgan was a shrewd businessman who had a great ability to see the bigger picture, find loopholes in policies, manipulate people to get what he wanted, and create plans to save businesses, and even entire governments, from ruin. It is these qualities that make him such an interesting figure in Titanic conspiracy theories.

J. Bruce Ismay

Joseph Bruce Ismay was the son of original White Star Line chairperson Thomas Bruce Ismay. The younger Ismay acquired the company after his father's death in 1899.

In 1902 J. Bruce Ismay sold White Star Line to J.P Morgan & Company during Morgan's creation of the International Mercantile Marine Company. He became the president of that company in 1904. As the president of a family company Ismay had a vested interest in making White Star Line look good.

Many stories from survivors had Ismay desperate to get Titanic up to full speed and make it to New York ahead of schedule. He was always looking for a way to get White Star Line some good press.

Ismay turned out to be one of the most controversial figures in Titanic history. Not only did he seem to want positive PR even if it meant putting passengers in danger, he was also the highest ranking White Star official to have survived the sinking. When the last lifeboat was ready to launch, First Officer Murdoch sent out a final call for women and children. When none responded he allowed men to board the boat.

First class passenger William Carter boarded, along with J. Bruce Ismay. As both a male and a higher up in the company's management, Ismay was basically expected to go down with the ship. The stigma of having not only survived the sinking, but actually having escaped on a lifeboat while other passengers were still waiting, followed him for the rest of his life. He was skewered in the press, being called names like the "coward of the Titanic" and "J. Brute Ismay".

The British inquiry into the sinking concluded that, "Had he not jumped in he would merely have added one more life, namely, his own, to the number of those lost." Still, he was criticized for his decision until his death in 1937.

E.J. Smith

Edward John Smith was commander of White Star Line's Olympic-class vessels. He captained Titanic's sister ship RMS Olympic, and was Titanic's captain for her doomed maiden voyage.

By all accounts he was a careful and extremely skilled captain. He had over 40 years' experience at sea before he took command of Titanic. It has been noted, however, that these Olympic-class ships were an entirely new kind of vessel. Nobody yet had experience with such large ships, and no amount of experience with ships half their size would prepare a person for the sheer power of a ship like Olympic or Titanic.

Captain Smith gained a new reputation as a slightly accident prone captain. Olympic's maiden voyage took the same route Titanic was meant to, from Southampton to New York. The journey was without incident until the ship got to the New York, and was being pulled into the pier by several tugboats. One of the boats got caught in the suction created by the massive Olympic and ended up colliding with the ship.

Later in 1911 Olympic had another incident with Smith as her captain, as the ship collided with the British naval cruiser HMS Hawke. Then, of course, there was the Titanic disaster. None of these incidences can be said to have been caused by a lack of skill on the part of Captain Smith. The ships were simply a new breed.

It is difficult to blame Smith for the collision with the iceberg. Many believe the captain should have slowed the ship down after hearing ice warnings. However, the night was still and clear, and it was not protocol to slow down for ice unless ice was actually visible. The inquiries into the sinking heard testimony from many passenger liner captains who all said they would have done the same things in Captain Smith's position.

Lord Mersey of the British inquiry concluded, "He made a mistake, a very grievous mistake, but one in which, in a face of the practice and of past experience, negligence cannot be said to have had any part; and in the absence of negligence it is, in my opinion, impossible to fix Captain Smith with blame."

All that being said, it must be remembered that no conspiracy plot to sink Titanic could possibly have gone ahead without the captain's knowledge, consent, and cooperation.

Stanley Lord

Captain Stanley Lord is another controversial figure in Titanic history who features prominently in most conspiracy theories of the sinking.

Lord was the captain of the SS Californian, the cargo ship that was in the vicinity of Titanic the night she sank, but that did not come to her aid. Lord's recounting of the incident on, what he called, "a most peculiar night" has been poured over and questioned for over a hundred years.

He claims the SS Californian attempted to signal the ship the crew saw in the distance with a Morse lamp, but that the mystery ship did not respond. Subsequent attempts to contact the ship also failed, so Captain Lord went to sleep. He was awoken by a crew member telling him the mystery ship had fired rockets. Lord asked what color they were, concluded they were company rockets, and went back to sleep.

It was not until later in the morning, when the Californian's wireless operator woke, that the ship's crew found out the vessel they had been attempting to signal was Titanic, and that she was in grave need of help. By that time, it was too late. Titanic had already sunk, and Carpathia was on the scene to rescue the survivors.

Captain Lord's inaction that night baffled the world, and continues to perplex historians and conspiracy theorists alike. Neither the British nor the American inquiries into the sinking saw fit to charge Lord with any offenses under the Merchant Shipping Acts. While many disapproved of his odd, borderline negligent behavior, it was not illegal.

Some claim that Captain Lord was simply an inexperienced captain. He just didn't want to restart the ship, navigate the ice-filled waters, and put the lives of his crew at risk, to help a ship that was not even in obvious distress.

All the same, Captain Lord's reputation suffered greatly after that night. A re-investigation by the British government, published in 1992, concluded that, had Californian moved to aid Titanic, it would have most likely gotten to the area at the same time as Carpathia. Unfortunately, Lord had died in 1962 and was not around to hear that his ship was not the lifesaver many claimed it could have been.

Now onto the theories.

It Wasn't Really Titanic

We know for certain that a massive ocean liner sank to the bottom of the Atlantic Ocean early in the morning of April 15th, 1912. That ship was reported to be White Star Line's newest vessel, RMS Titanic. But was it really Titanic that sank that morning? Mounting evidence suggests it was actually a different White Star Line ship that took the plunge into the icy waters.

Titanic's sister ship, the RMS Olympic, was on its fifth voyage in 1911 when it collided with a British naval cruiser, the HMS Hawke. Olympic sustained significant damage. An inquiry into the incident concluded that the Olympic was entirely at fault. Apparently the water displacement of the ship created a suction that pulled Hawke into Olympic, causing the damage. White Star Line received no insurance money, or financial aid of any kind to fix the ship.

The company was left to pay the legal bills from the collision, and the costs of repairing Olympic completely out of pocket. It was likely that Olympic would not even pass any upcoming inspections with the damage it sustained. The massive ship was essentially scrap metal.

White Star also had the rest of Titanic still to build. All the costs were adding up, and the company was facing a huge financial disaster. They had to find a way to not have to completely repair the damaged ship, and still be able to launch Titanic unscathed and on schedule.

The theory goes that J.P Morgan, owner of White Star, decided to have the damaged RMS Olympic mocked up to look like Titanic. It would then be deliberately damaged so White Star could collect the much-needed insurance money that would help keep the company afloat. As an added public relations bonus, Morgan planned to save everyone aboard from the wreckage.

This theory doesn't come completely out of left field. It is obvious that the company took a financial hit after being burdened with the blame for the Olympic collision, but that is far from the only evidence for deliberately damaging the ship.

First, Titanic was not nearly at capacity when it set sail. The maiden voyage of a luxurious ocean liner with as much press as Titanic should have been easy to fill. In fact, because of the coal strike, other ships were cancelling their journeys and transferring their passengers to Titanic. Titanic was one of the few ships that had secured enough coal for its voyage, and was one of the comparatively few passenger liners even making the journey to America at the time. The ship should have had far more passengers aboard. Instead only about half the cabins were occupied.

Similarly, it was oddly difficult to staff the ship with men to work in the boiler room. Boilermen actually resigned, or did not sign on again, after the trip from the shipyard in Belfast to the launching docks in Southampton. Considering there was a coal strike happening at the time, making such jobs scarce, the competition for these positions should have been fierce.

Both the lack of passengers and the inability to find staff suggest there were rumors circulating about the insurance scam that made people uneasy about getting on the ship. This is further backed up by the fact that over fifty high profile guests cancelled their voyages on Titanic shortly before the ship was meant to set sail.

These guests included many of Morgan's wealthy colleagues who had less-than-convincing reasons for cancelling. Clay Frick, industrialist and steel magnate, cancelled the voyage of his entire family and their entourage because of his wife's sprained ankle.

George Vanderbilt III, a businessman and an important figure in the transportation industries of America, also cancelled his voyage with his wife just one day before the ship left Southampton. He sent one of their servants, Frederick Wheeler, ahead to America on Titanic with the Vanderbilt's luggage. Wheeler did not survive the sinking. It is unclear what the Vanderbilt's reason for cancelling was, or what they planned to do without their luggage until they could catch another ship across the ocean.

Milton Hershey, founder of the Hershey Chocolate Company, also cancelled his voyage with his wife due to business matters. They travelled back to America on the German luxury liner, SS Amerika. The cheque Hershey wrote to White Star Line for his first class cabin is now on display at the Hershey museum.

Even J.P Morgan himself cancelled his trip on his company's own ocean liner. He claimed to be too ill to travel, and also wanted to accompany his art collection home from Paris. He was seen a few days later in France, in what seemed to be perfect health, enjoying the sun with his mistress.

Additionally, Morgan had valuable bronze statues removed from the ship before the voyage. Why cancel a voyage on, and remove valuables from, a ship that plans to dock safely in New York?

There is also physical evidence that the ship that set sail from the Southampton dock was not actually Titanic. Diagrams of Olympic's damage that were released by shipbuilders

Harland and Wolff show that the damage sustained by Olympic on her forward compartments almost exactly matches the damage that is meant to have sunk Titanic. The two ships were either coincidentally damaged in the exact same way, or they were actually the same ship.

The physical evidence does not stop there. According to maritime history enthusiasts who have compared photos of Titanic and Olympic at different stages in the ships' lifetimes, Olympic began to change after her accident. As Olympic was being repaired from the collision she suddenly took on a distinctive porthole arrangement she didn't have when she first set sail. Olympic's portholes, once evenly spaced, now matched the unique, unevenly spaced pattern of Titanic's.

So people were reluctant to board Titanic, and her sister ship Olympic was starting to look more like her twin. It sounds suspicious, but how could White Star Line switch two massive ocean liners without anyone noticing?

In March of 1912 Olympic and Titanic were sharing the one dry dock at the Belfast shipyard. Titanic was allegedly being finished, and Olympic was getting her final repairs. Because the ships had to keep moving back and forth, sharing the single dock, a switch could have easily been made with only the most astute observer realizing what had happened.

Not much inside the ship had to be changed, either. Most of the odds and ends of White Star ships were stamped, not with the name of the ship, but with the White Star logo. The ships' accoutrements were basically made to be interchangeable.

On the day of the maiden voyage observers noticed that whichever ship left the dock that day was moving in a way consistent with the damaged sustained by Olympic. Several survivors noted that the ship listed port. In fact, the ship almost collided with another vessel upon its launch. This has been put down to the enormous pull Titanic created in the water due to her size, but could also have something to do with the fact the ship was moving erratically.

The strangeness continued at the time of the sinking. Titanic only had white rockets on board, and used these to signal nearby ships for help. White rockets were generally used to illuminate a path, to signal a greeting to other ships at night, or simply as company signals, made to inform other ships of the company the ship belongs to.

According to maritime procedure in 1912 these rockets could have been used in a distress call if they had been fired at intervals of one minute. However, Titanic did not send up her rockets in this manner.

The SS Californian, a ship that was in the area that morning, saw the white flares Titanic sent up, but thought little of them as they were not fired in a manner that would signal the ship needed help. Captain Lord of the Californian assumed Titanic's rockets were company signals.

Other means of signaling for help also fell short. The distress signal sent over the ship's wires wasn't sent until 47 minutes after the impact with the iceberg. It also initially gave the wrong location, saying Titanic was 13 miles from where she actually was. Some take this to mean someone aboard was delaying calling for help until they were sure the plan was going smoothly and the ship was certainly damaged. It could also indicate that the damage to the ship was much more severe than it was meant to be.

It is possible that the crew was not expecting to have to call for help after the collision. The plan may have been to damage the ship, not fully sink it. After all, having two operational passenger liners would be much more lucrative for the company than having one lying on the ocean floor. Only when it became clear that the damage to the ship would be fatal did the crew feel the need to send out signals for help.

Even more confusion was happening back on land. Headlines and announcements of the incident reported that everyone had survived the disaster, and even that the ship was still afloat. The Evening Sun's April 15th front page headline read, "All Saved From Titanic After Collision", with the story saying "...Liner is being towed to Halifax after smashing into an iceberg".

Some have attempted to explain this away by saying it was simply a case of crossed wires. A wireless message that was meant to say, "Are all Titanic's passengers safe?" accidentally came out as "All Titanic's passengers safe." However, this does not explain why newspapers reported that

Titanic was still afloat and being taken to Halifax. This could be indicative of a prefabricated release of information that gave details of the original plan to simply damage- not entirely sink-the ship, and to save all passengers on board.

There is also a strange story that the surviving crew were taken aside by a member of the British government and a high ranking official from White Star Line when survivors got back to land. According to one man, the crew were made to sign a document under the Official Secrets Act of 1911 saying they would not talk about the incident.

From the cancellations of important figures before setting sail, to the odd announcements that all passengers were safe, almost every step of the maiden voyage of Titanic pointed to something strange going on in the upper levels of White Star Line's management. Did J.P Morgan switch Titanic out for Olympic? Did he want to deliberately re-damage Olympic to collect the insurance money that would save his company? Did that plan go horribly wrong forcing the crew to have to think on their feet and completely improvise a rescue scenario? And was the crew then sworn to secrecy to protect J.P Morgan and White Star Line?

A German U-Boat Sank Titanic

Another theory of why Titanic actually sank can also be tied to insurance fraud, but has its roots in the mounting political tension between Germany and Britain before World War I.

This theory suggests that a German submarine (called unterseeboot in German, or U-boat for short) torpedoed the ship, causing it to sink. Reasoning for this has also been linked to White Star Line's financial troubles, and J.P Morgan's need to collect the insurance money he was denied after the Olympic wreck. Allegedly the captain of the U-boat in question was related to one of

Titanic's owners, and agreed to take part in the insurance scam.

Another reason behind this theory is simply a terrorist strike by Germany against Britain amid the rising tension that eventually led to war. Another passenger ship, Lusitania, was known to have been sunk by a German U-boat three years later, in 1915, confirming for some that Titanic could have met the same fate.

While the various reasonings behind this theory are pretty shaky there is actually some evidence that there was another mysterious sea craft in the water that night.

Crew members reported hearing four loud explosion-like bangs deep within the ship *after* the impact with the iceberg. Some crew also reported seeing an unidentified vessel in the water about 5 miles from Titanic at the time of the alleged impact.

Passengers on deck waiting for lifeboats saw lights in the distance between Titanic and where Californian was known to be at the time. Some have speculated that the mystery ship was Samson, a Norwegian seal hunting ship that did not come to the aid of Titanic because it was illegally hunting in that area. However, Samson's records show that it was at the fishing port of Isafjordhur, 3000 miles away, on both April 6th, and April 20th. Even if Samson had made the journey at top speed the Norwegian ship was much too far away at that time to have made the journey to where Titanic was that morning.

The idea that a German U-boat had anything to do with the sinking was more than likely just born out of the political tensions in the world at the time. There is not much actual evidence for Germany's involvement in a plot to sink the ship either for J.P Morgan, or as a terrorist act against Britain. Still, the idea of a mystery ship persists. What was the vessel both passengers and crew saw in the distance that morning, and did it have anything to do with the sinking?

The Californian Controversy

The existence of the ship SS Californian in the vicinity of Titanic on the night she sank is one of the most controversial pieces of that night's complicated puzzle.

The Californian was a Leyland Line cargo steamer travelling from Liverpool to Boston. Though it had room for passengers, it was not carrying any at the time. It's cargo consisted only of blankets and sweaters. These are both suspicious details. The Californian was traveling across the Atlantic in the middle of a coal strike with no passengers, and no urgent cargo. Ships back in Britain were needing to cancel their voyages and transfer their passengers to other liners due to a lack of coal, yet Californian was freely sailing.

Late in the evening on April 14th the ship found itself in some ice fields. The inexperienced Captain Stanley Lord decided to stop for the night and navigate the ice in the morning. Again, this seems awfully convenient. A ship devoid of passengers happens to be spending the night just a few miles from where a rescue ship will be desperately needed.

According to crew accounts of the night, Third Officer Charles Groves saw Titanic in the distance at around 11pm. He thought the ship to be 10-12 miles away. Captain Lord asked him to contact the ship with a Morse lamp and inform it of the ice that Californian had encountered. Titanic did not respond.

Wireless operator Cyril Evans attempted to contact Titanic but was allegedly told "Shut up! Shut up! I am busy. I am working to communicate with Cape Race" by Titanic wireless operator Jack Phillips. Apparently the two ships were too close to one another and Evans' message came in extremely loud. Evans continued to listen to Titanic for a while, but went to sleep shortly after the communication with Phillips.

Another attempt was made by crew member James Gibson to signal Titanic with a Morse lamp. Again he did not receive a coherent reply. He thought he saw a light on the ship respond, but concluded it was just a flickering ship light, not a Morse lamp.

Second Officer Herbert Stone was on deck when Titanic fired the first five rockets she sent up that night. Gibson soon joined him and the two men watched as three more white rockets came up from the ship. Only after the eight rockets went up was Captain Lord informed of the possible distress signal. Lord just asked about the color of the rockets, and gave no further instruction to his crew.

Chief Officer George Stewart took over watch at 4am, at which point he was told of the events of the night. Looking out at the location of the mystery ship, he and Second Officer Herbert Stone saw a different ship to the one they had been attempting to signal the previous night.

Only then did Evans turn on his equipment again and learn that Titanic had been signaling for help. By that time Titanic had already sunk. The different ship Stewart and Stone saw was Carpathia attempting to save the lives of Titanic's passengers.

The justification for Captain Lord's disinterest in Titanic's rocket signals has been hotly debated since that night. Supporters of the captain's inaction claim that he didn't do anything wrong. He asked for the color of the rockets that this mystery ship sent up and, upon hearing they were white, decided the ship was simply signaling a greeting.

At the time there was not actually one agreed upon way to signal other ships in times of distress. Generally, though, flares or rockets should be set off at one minute intervals.

Titanic did not fire her rockets in that manner. The Californian crew could have been confused as to what Titanic's intention for firing the rockets was. However, company signals were strictly regimented, and it did not make sense that Titanic, or any other ship in the area, would be sending up a greeting at that time.

Considering the fact that any signal that could not be definitely interpreted as a company greeting should have been construed as a distress signal, it becomes clear that Californian should have come to Titanic's aid that night.

Author Leslie Reade's book *The Ship That Stood Still* is a detailed look into Californian's actions that night. He went through all maritime signals that were known and agreed upon at the time and concluded that there was no way Californian should have mistaken Titanic's rockets for a greeting. Reade wrote, "In 1912 company signals were so rarely used on the high seas that it was highly unreasonable for any master to think that a reported rocket (or rockets) would have been a company signal."

The U.S inquiry into the Titanic sinking concluded that Californian saw Titanic's signals and, "failed to respond to them in accordance with humanity, international usage, and requirements of law." The British inquiry also laid some of the blame for the magnitude of the disaster at the feet of Captain Lord, and Californian's crew. None of the men were officially charged, but their negligence was certainly noted.

Captain Lord's inaction that night could possibly be explained away by the confusion over ship signals. There is also a popular theory that the crew thought they saw a small ship 6 miles away, rather than a large ship 12 miles away. This would explain why Californian did not hear the rockets sent up by Titanic, and why the Morse lamp received no reply, making the next steps they should take unclear.

These theories do not explain the damning evidence of a cover-up that came later. Californian's official logbooks did not mention either rockets or mystery ships. The scrap log on which crew members write details of the journey that is supposed to later make up the official log, had mysteriously disappeared.

The lack of official (or unofficial) notes on Californian's encounter with Titanic cannot just be put down to inefficient record keeping. An inaccurate message was sent from the nearby Olympic to land saying that Californian had picked up bodies on her way to Boston. Press was waiting for the ship when she arrived. Captain Lord told Boston newspapers that Californian, "had sighted no rockets or other signals of distress" and that "nothing of the kind was seen by [Officer Stewart] or any of the men who were on watch with him."

Californian's presence in the water that night, and the subsequent actions of the captain and crew can be taken two ways: it was a simple mistake by an inexperienced captain, or it was a sinister cover-up.

Either Captain Lord was embarrassed by his decision to not help Titanic and decided to cover up the fact that his ship could have come to her aid; or Californian was part of an insurance scam plot that went horribly awry.

Could Californian have been part of J.P Morgan's plan to damage Titanic for the insurance money? Some details line up with a possible involvement in a White Star insurance scam.

Californian was part of the Leyland Line of ships. Leyland was owned by the same people who owned Titanic's White Star Line. If J.P Morgan needed a ship to perform a rescue he would have had the ability to recruit a ship and a willing captain from a Leyland liner.

No passengers were aboard Californian at the time of its voyage. This could potentially point to the fact that the ship was expecting to pick up some passengers during its journey. As previously noted, having a completely empty ship so close to where Titanic sank seems very convenient.

So why did Captain Lord not come to Titanic's aid?

Both the confusion over the rocket signals, and the distance of the ship could explain why Californian did not go to the ship's rescue. The crew was unsure whether the ship in the distance was a small ship approximately 6 miles away, or a large ship approximately 12 miles away. If Lord was waiting for a ship of Titanic's size to signal them he would not have moved to help a smaller, closer ship.

In Lord's testimony to the US inquiry he said the wireless operator told him it was Titanic in the distance, to which Lord replied "This is not the Titanic; there is no doubt about it." He seemed so sure it was not Titanic, and was inexplicably reluctant to help whatever ship it may have been. It seems that Lord thought he knew what to look for when looking out for Titanic, and couldn't risk being busy with another ship when the time came to help Titanic.

The fact that Lord's sole interest seemed to be the color of the rockets is also odd. Knowing that white rockets fired in a particular way could have been a distress signal in 1912, it is unusual that the captain would ignore this. Perhaps he was waiting for a different color rocket before going to help the passengers of the ship he was supposed to aid.

This does not explain why Titanic never sent up a rocket that was any color other than white. If Captain Lord was waiting for a different color before moving to help the ship's passengers, Titanic should have sent up that color.

Perhaps Lord was simply so convinced that the ship was not Titanic that he needed an excuse to not go to the mystery ship's side. Asking about the color of the rockets and appearing convinced they were just company signals excused his decision to ignore what was happening.

The inaction might also indicate Captain Lord's reluctance to participate in Morgan's plot. Perhaps he initially agreed to help Morgan collect on the insurance, but no longer wanted to be involved in the plan when the time came. That would explain the incorrect logs and Lord's flawed statements to the press. After all, Lord was later quoted as saying, "you never mistake a distress rocket." So why did he?

Was the SS Californian part of the plot to save passengers after deliberately damaging Titanic? Was Lord waiting for a different signal before helping? Did he change his mind about being involved? Why did Californian's logs not mention any signals or other ships? And why did Captain Lord initially lie to the press about seeing them?

A Dark Family Secret

In 2010 a new theory for the sinking arose when Lady Louise Patten revealed a long-held family secret to the world. She claims that she had learned her grandfather, Titanic's Second Officer Charles Lightoller, knew who was actually responsible for Titanic hitting the iceberg that night.

Lightoller went down with the ship but was subsequently rescued by a lifeboat, and survived to pass on the tale to his family.

Lightoller alleges that the man in charge of steering Titanic that night, Robert Hitchens, panicked when he saw the ice and realized the danger the ship was in. He accidentally steered Titanic in the wrong direction, making it collide with the iceberg. Patten says the error came from the differences between the steering on sailing ships and steam ships.

Sailing ships worked on Tiller Orders. This meant that you turned the tiller in the opposite direction of where you wanted to go. If you wanted to go right, you'd turn the tiller left. Steam ships, though, worked on Rudder Orders, a more intuitive system where you turned the rudder in the direction you wanted to go.

Apparently in the North Atlantic at the time, they were still using Tiller Orders for all ships. Even though Titanic was a steamship, when First Officer William Murdoch gave the command that would steer the ship away from danger, he gave it in Tiller Orders. Hitchens, having been trained to steer in

Rudder Orders, turned the ship the wrong way. By the time anyone noticed the mistake it was too late to correct the course.

This incident had remained a secret for almost 100 years, as the family did not want to sully the good name of Patten's grandfather, or have a hand in changing the public opinion of what actually happened to the famous ship.

It is an interesting theory, but it doesn't change the history that much. Titanic, whether by a failure to see what was ahead, or by a human steering error, hit the iceberg by accident and sank into the ocean. Regardless of the reason, it would still have been an accident.

However, Patten claims that is not where the cover-up ends.

J. Bruce Ismay was known to want to get to New York ahead of schedule. It would be a real PR boost for White Star Line, which the company desperately needed. Patten alleges that Ismay sent out an order for the ship to go slow ahead after it struck the iceberg. This action put pressure on the hull and ended up being the reason the watertight compartments flooded, leading to the sinking.

If Titanic had stayed still instead, the watertight hull compartments would not have been breached, and the damage to the ship would not have been nearly as significant. Titanic would most likely have stayed afloat until the rescue ships came. Everyone aboard would have survived. However, that would mean the ship being towed into New York, rather than making a triumphant and impressive voyage to the pier.

That would have been a PR disaster Ismay was just not willing to let happen. Ismay and White Star Line could not risk their newest, most luxurious ship looking weak and incapable of safe travel. Especially right on the heels of the Olympic's collision with HMS Hawke. White Star was already in trouble, and having Titanic towed pitifully into New York would have been the final nail in the coffin.

It was Ismay's desperate need for good PR for White Star that ultimately doomed the ship and ended so many lives. Patten claims Ismay then told her grandfather to keep quiet about his knowledge of who was really responsible for the sinking. If White Star's insurance company found out that the damage was due to human error, they would not receive any insurance money.

White Star Line could not afford to have to foot the bills for repairs on two of their Olympic-class ocean liners, and have to keep Titanic out of commission until she was repaired. They desperately needed the insurance money, or White Star would go under and many men would lose their livelihoods.

Lightoller and Ismay, the only two men in the know who survived the sinking, agreed to cover-up the real reason Titanic hit the iceberg to protect the company, and protect the jobs of countless men.

Significant Ship Damage Was Ignored

It is a well-known fact that Titanic was on fire when she left the shipyard in Belfast to travel to the loading docks in Southampton. Coalmen on the ship estimate the fire could have started as early as April 2nd, over a week before Titanic boarded passengers and began her maiden voyage.

The fire started in coal room 6, as the fuel spontaneously caught fire and could have reached 1000 degrees Celsius. Ship workers claim it is not unusual for large piles of coal to catch fire on their own. They are normally put out by simply shoveling the coal into a furnace, which usually has no adverse effect on the ship.

On Titanic, though, getting rid of the burning coal by shoveling it into the engine may have sealed her fate.

The fire was said to have significantly weakened the exact spot where the iceberg struck. At an inquiry hearing after the sinking one worker, Fireman Charles Hendrickson, described area where the fire was as "dented a bit" and "warped". He claimed to have made cosmetic repairs to the inside of the ship to hide the fact that there was ever a fire.

Every effort was made by White Star Line management to downplay the severity of the fire. An inspector who was aboard the ship for three days prior to the maiden voyage was not even informed of the fire, and workers were told to basically ignore its existence.

In 2012, photographs from a private collection surfaced showing Titanic at the dock before it set sail. They show what is confirmed to be a 30-foot blemish on the starboard side, exactly where the ship hit the iceberg. Titanic was allegedly backed into the dock to hide the blemish from passengers. White Star Line couldn't have more passengers cancelling their voyages at the last minute due to concerns over the ship's safety.

White Star Line also could not afford any more delay in launching ship. If the inspector had been told of the fire, and how it weakened the ship's hull, he most likely would not have signed off on the ship taking its maiden voyage. With the bills from the Olympic collision still to pay, the company was in trouble. White Star needed Titanic to be fully operational.

It was highly unlikely that the weakened hull would cause a problem. Even if Titanic was involved in a collision, and the hull was punctured, the watertight compartments would protect the ship from sinking. After all, Titanic could stay afloat with any two compartments, or all three forward compartments flooded. The chances of that kind of damage were very slim. White Star could risk sending Titanic out onto the ocean with the fire damage if it meant they could save the company.

There were rumors that Captain E.J Smith was looking to win the Blue Riband for the fastest Atlantic crossing, causing him to journey at a reckless speed for most of the voyage. This is not true. The Mauretania held the record at the time and nobody believed Titanic could possibly be faster than that ship. She simply wasn't built that way.

However, Captain Smith, at the urging of J. Bruce Ismay, may have been attempting to beat Olympic's maiden voyage crossing time. A surviving passenger, Elizabeth Lines, claimed she overheard Ismay excitedly talking about the speed at which Titanic was moving. She alleges he told the captain, "We will beat the Olympic and get into New York on Tuesday."

Titanic was supposed to arrive in New York on Wednesday morning. Getting there ahead of schedule would have been a great PR boost for White Star, so there was definite incentive for the ship to go as fast as possible.

This, plus the fact they were already going faster than necessary because of the coal being shoveled into the engine from the coal fire, meant Titanic was travelling at an immense speed when it approached and collided with the iceberg. It had not quite yet reached full speed, but the ship was travelling faster than it had the entire voyage, and was certainly on her way to full speed.

The great speed meant two things that ultimately doomed the ship. First, the lookouts didn't have enough time to properly react to seeing the iceberg. Had Titanic been going slower they would have seen the ice sooner, and been able to correct the course of the ship to avoid impact. Second, if the ship were going slower the force of the impact would have been smaller, causing less damage, and most likely keeping the ship afloat until everyone on board could be rescued.

As it happened, though, the ship's speed made for a tremendously forceful impact. Also, already weakened by the coal fire, the hull was easily penetrable.

It wasn't only the impact with the iceberg that sunk Titanic. Significant ship damage from the coal fire was covered up and largely ignored in order to launch Titanic on time. The damage incurred may not have been so significant or fatal had the fire been seen to, or had the inspector been told of it.

Titanic also may not have been going almost top speed when it hit iceberg if J.Bruce Ismay didn't want to break a record. Basically, if all safety precautions were followed, Titanic would not have sunk, but profit and PR were more important than safety.

Assassinations

In the early 1900's, White Star Line owner J.P. Morgan wanted the U.S to move away from its unstable, unfocused financial system. At the time the American economy was rife with financial panics and bank closures. At the time it was not all that safe, or smart, for foreign or domestic investors to back American industries. The economy was flagging. The government needed a real solution that would not only fix their immediate financial woes, but ensure a stable economic future as well.

A centralized bank is an independent institution that creates monetary policy for the government, watches over the economy, and generally creates a more stable economic environment for a country. Essentially it controls a country's money supply. It is the government's bank, and as such, wields enormous power in the country.

Every other major economy in the world at the time was backed by a centralized bank, and Morgan was pushing for America to follow suit, using his own wealth as part of the beginning of the system.

In both 1893 and 1907, J.P. Morgan used his immense fortune to almost single-handedly pull the United States economy away from the brink of a depression. He injected money into the U.S Treasury and into various stocks of big companies. After the near disaster of 1907, the government had no choice but to move to create a centralized banking system. After all, there would not always be a J.P. Morgan around to bail the government out.

They needed a permanent stable system in place.

Three extremely wealthy and influential men aboard Titanic allegedly opposed the creation of this centralized bank, now known as the Federal Reserve.

Benjamin Guggenheim was a businessman, president of the International Steam Pump Company, heir to the Guggenheim fortune, and a known philanderer. He was travelling with his mistress, Léontine Aubart, her maid, Emma Sägesser, and his valet, Victor Giglio. After the collision with the iceberg, the women in the party boarded lifeboat 9, but Guggenheim and Giglio refused a space on the boat. Guggenheim was told, considering his wealth, nobody would object to him boarding a lifeboat with his mistress. Again he refused.

Guggenheim and Giglio wore their best evening clothes and waited to go down with the ship. Guggenheim was quoted as saying, "We've dressed in our best, and are prepared to go down like gentlemen. There is grave doubt that the men will get off. I am willing to remain and play the man's game if there are not enough boats for more than the women and children. I won't die here like a beast. Tell my wife I played the game out straight and to the end. No woman shall be left aboard this ship because Ben Guggenheim was a coward."

Isidor Straus was related to Ben Guggenheim by marriage. He was co-owner of Macy's department store, and was a former member of the U.S House of Representatives. Straus was travelling with his wife, Ida. Like Guggenheim, Straus refused to get into a lifeboat, even though there was room. He said, "I will not go before the other men."

Ida refused to be separated from her husband. After already securing a place in lifeboat 8, she stepped out of the boat, joined her husband on the deck and told him, "As we lived, so will we die, together."

John Jacob Astor IV was a decorated military man and a real estate mogul. He was the richest man aboard Titanic, and rumored to be one of the richest men in the world. Astor built the Astoria Hotel in New York in 1897, and merged it with his cousin's hotel, the Waldorf, to create the Waldorf-Astoria. The five-star luxury hotel would soon house the official American inquiry into the sinking of the Titanic.

Astor was on board Titanic returning from his honeymoon to Egypt and Italy with his pregnant second wife, Madeleine Force.

Initially Astor was not convinced of the severity of the disaster. He claimed, "we are safer here than in that little boat." After a talk with Captain Smith he was convinced to get his wife into a lifeboat. Astor attempted to board the boat with her was but was refused. The attendant told him they were not loading men until all the women were accounted for. Archibald Gracie said Astor, "bore the refusal bravely and resignedly." Astor died when the ship went down. His body was found a week later.

All three men were wildly influential in the American economy, all were allegedly opposed the creation of the Federal Reserve, and all died when Titanic sank. Some theorize that J.P Morgan had Titanic deliberately sunk to get rid of opposition to the centralized banking system that would give him so much power over the American economy.

Considering the lengths wealthy people go to in order to protect their assets and keep their power, an assassination plot is not so hard to believe. Especially when you add the fact that Morgan and several wealthy colleagues cancelled their voyages shortly before Titanic set sail. If it is true that these men were standing in Morgan's way, then there must have been less opposition to the creation of a central bank after the sinking.

Is it just a coincidence that America's centralized bank, the Federal Reserve, was created by President Woodrow Wilson just one year after the sinking? Did J.P Morgan tell his friends of an assassination plot to get rid of dissenters of the Federal Reserve? Did Morgan and his influential friends cancel their voyages to stay safe, and eventually influence the government to create the Federal Reserve?

The Paranormal

Rumors of strange, and even paranormal, happenings have plagued Titanic since before it even set sail. The following are not necessarily conspiracy theories as to why Titanic sank, but rather seemingly otherworldly occurrences that offer an alternative look into why Titanic may have faced such bad luck.

Curses

The tale of the mummy's curse has been passed on as a reason for the sinking since almost immediately after the ship went down. On the night of April 12th 1912, journalist, fiction writer, and activist William Thomas Stead, along with his friend Douglas

Murray, told his fellow dinner companions on Titanic a story about an Egyptian mummy, the princess of Amen-Ra, that brought death and destruction wherever it went.

According to Stead, the princess' sarcophagus was dug up in Luxor in the 1890's, and sold to four Englishmen. Each of the buyers suffered misfortunes. Two of the men died, one lost his entire fortune, and the last became ill, lost his job, and was forced to live on the street.

Another English man bought the coffin but, after his family was injured and his house caught fire, the man donated the mummy to the British Museum. The mummy continued to bring death and destruction as she terrorized museum workers and their families. Eventually the museum wanted to get rid of this horrible cursed object.

Princess Amen-Ra and her sarcophagus were bought by a private collector who tried to have the evil exorcised from it. He was told by the famous occultist Madame Helena Blavatsky that this was impossible; the mummy would always be evil.

An American archaeologist heard of the mummy and her history of rampant destruction. Not believing the rumors, or wanting to see for himself, the man paid to have the sarcophagus shipped from England to America. The sarcophagus was loaded onto Titanic and set off for its new home, dooming the ship to be another casualty of Amen-Ra's curse.

Stead and Murray had come up with the mummy's tale by conflating a ghost story they had written, with the anguished image on the coffin lid of the Priestess of Amun in the Egypt Room of the British Museum. They thought the image depicted such a tortured soul that her spirit was bound to be wandering the Earth and causing destruction.

Frederic Seward was the only person at the table with Stead that night who survived the disaster. He recounted the horror story many times, often with his own embellishments. In time people actually believed the mummy was on board Titanic that night, and even that Stead himself was the one who brought it there. The story got stranger and stranger the more it was told. It was eventually suggested the mummy somehow got rescued on a lifeboat and made its way back to England, only to gain passage on Lusitania, another doomed vessel.

Titanic's cargo manifest makes no mention of a mummy on board, or any other dead body for that matter. Most people believe Stead's story, told time and again by Seward, then passed on by those who heard it from him, got wrapped up in the memories of the survivors who heard it, and became part of the history of the ship.

However, there isn't even an accurate number for how many passengers were on the ship, or for how many died in the sinking. If the passenger lists were so out of date and confusing, isn't it at least a little possible that the cargo manifest was also inaccurate? Could there have been a malicious spirit aboard the ship that continued to bring destruction?

Perhaps it wasn't the evil spirit of an ancient Egyptian princess, but that of a man that led to Titanic's sinking. At least one man, James Dobbins, died during the building of Titanic. There were also rumors that a man was accidentally sealed into the ship's hull during construction.

This claim has been refuted by White Star Line, but it cannot be denied that a shipyard in the early 1900s would have been a hectic and dangerous place to work. There were more than likely countless injuries sustained by workers while building Titanic, and the many ships that came through the yard before her. Could an old spirit have latched onto the new ship?

Evil spirits aren't the only things that could have cursed Titanic. There is a persistent idea that Titanic was cursed because the traditional champagne bottle used to christen ships at the time didn't break on its hull. This was supposed to be a bad omen for the ship. In actuality, White Star Line didn't christen any of its ships this way. The bottle didn't break because it never existed. But is not christening the ship at all what doomed Titanic instead?

White Star's two other Olympic-class liners, of which Titanic was a part, also met with bad luck in their careers. RMS Olympic collided with HMS Hawke on its fifth voyage in 1911. This dealt a substantial financial blow to the company, and delayed the launch of Titanic for several weeks as materials from that build had to be repurposed to fix Olympic.

The third Olympic-class liner, HMHS Britannic, met a similar fate to Titanic. She hit an underwater mine and was wrecked in 1916, less than one year after her completion. Thirty people died and the ship was lost for good.

Not one White Star passenger liner was christened in the traditional way, and not one made it a year without a significant disaster. A botched christening may be a bad omen, but it would seem that no christening at all is fatal.

Predictions

W.T Stead, the man who started the mummy's curse rumor that persists to this day, also wrote two stories that seemed to predict the sinking, and show the anxieties he must have had about boarding Titanic.

Stead wrote *How the Mail Steamer Went Down in Mid Atlantic, by a Survivor* in 1886. It was published in the Pall Mall Gazette. The story tells of a ship that hits another sea vessel during a foggy night. The ship begins to sink, and there ensues a mad, panicked dash of passengers to the lifeboats. It quickly becomes apparent that there aren't enough lifeboats to save everyone aboard. Men force their way into boats, and the crew must use guns to try and keep order and prevent a riot from happening.

Stead also wrote the story *From the Old World to the New,* in 1892. It was also about a maritime disaster. In it a ship must come to the aid of another vessel that has collided with an iceberg. Putting the two stories together, it is almost as of Stead knew what awaited him in his future.

Of the 1886 story, Stead said, "This is exactly what might take place and will take place if liners are sent to sea short of boats." His warning was not heeded, and his story came to life on the night of the Titanic disaster.

Interestingly, Stead was also said to have a lifelong feeling that he would die by either lynching or drowning. Stead went down with the ship after heroically helping many women and children into lifeboats, and giving up his lifejacket to another passenger.

He is presumed to have drowned, though his body was never recovered.

Stead was for from the only person to have an eerie premonition about Titanic's maiden voyage. On the night of April 11th, 1912, a young Scottish girl, Jessie Sayre had an awful vision. She was dying, and was in an extremely delirious state when she told bystanders that she saw a large ship sinking into the ocean, and a man named Wally playing the fiddle as it went down. The violinist and bandleader on Titanic was named Wallace Hartley. He and his band are known to have played on the deck while lifeboats were being loaded.

Edith Russell, who ended up surviving the disaster, claimed in a letter before she set sail, "I cannot get over my feeling of depression and premonition of trouble."

Similarly, Robertha Watt sat at tea with some fellow passengers when one woman decided to read the tea leaves in her cup. This was a popular fortune telling parlor trick at the time. A person was meant to be able to tell the someone's future by analyzing the residual leaves in their teacup. In one cup the fortune teller saw something frightening. She said, "I can't see anything, it's like there was just a blank wall and nothing beyond."

Perhaps the most startling paranormal occurrence surrounding Titanic is that the sinking was predicted by a writer, in alarmingly similar detail, 14 years before it happened. In 1898 Morgan Robertson wrote a novella entitled *Futility, or the Wreck of the*

Titan. In it, Robertson describes the doomed voyage of a massive ocean liner named Titan. The ship, equipped with the same revolutionary watertight compartments found on Titanic, strikes an iceberg on a still April night. Due to a lack of lifeboats, many passengers on Titan lost their lives in the sinking.

Not all the details of Robertson's story match that of Titanic so closely, but the ones that do match are eerie. Robertson even seemed to predict the month the disaster would take place. The stories are so similar that some think J.P Morgan used *Futility* as the template for the Titanic sinking in an insurance scam plot. Most, though, believe it was an ominous prediction of the horror that was to befall the passengers of Titanic just 14 years later.

Conclusion

We may never really know what happened
to Titanic. The evidence of a conspiracy plot
may be buried with her at the bottom of the
ocean, or in the hearts of the conspirators
themselves.

We do, however, know some details about
Titanic history that make these conspiracy
theories all the more believable.

RMS Olympic sustained significant damage
on a 1911 voyage that, because of a lack of
insurance money, put White Star Line in
financial trouble. J.P Morgan, J. Bruce Ismay,
and White Star Line could not afford another
financial, or public relations disaster. The
company was on the verge of ruin.

J.P Morgan, the relatively new owner of White Star Line, was an expert at getting companies out of tight financial spots, and may have been able to fix a deliberate damaging of a ship in order to collect on the insurance money he felt the company deserved from the Olympic collision.

It is also a fairly well documented fact that J. Bruce Ismay was so wrapped up in White Star's reputation that he would have done anything for the company to be seen in a positive light, and wanted to avoid negative press at all costs. This led him to want to get Titanic to New York as early as possible by going as fast as possible, and, according to Lady Patten, caused him to order the ship forward after the collision with the iceberg, despite the damage it was sure to cause.

It cannot be denied that there were a large number of odd occurrences surrounding the building, launching, and sinking of Titanic. Whether you believe the official account of the sinking, or are open to other possibilities, it certainly seems clear that the higher ups in White Star Line's management had both the motive and opportunity to either stage a sinking, or to cover up the accidents that may have befallen the ship due to negligence.

There are, as yet, no plans to raise the wreck of the Titanic, that was found by Dr. Robert Ballard in 1985. The former ship is not in good condition and it's certainly not getting any better. The wreck is actually being slowly eaten by marine organisms that are creating what Ballard refers to as "rusticles", or rust icicles.

Titanic's two major parts are 1,970 feet apart, and each part has its own 2,000-foot-long debris field. Also, because they are sitting at the bottom of the ocean, each piece is experiencing 6,000 pounds of pressure per square inch. It would not be practical or profitable for anyone to attempt to resurrect the rusted remains. Parts may be brought to the surface piecemeal, but Titanic will most likely remain on the ocean floor until she has completely deteriorated.

Perhaps that is exactly how the men who sank her wanted it.

Printed in Great Britain
by Amazon